S0-ARG-051

# OLD KING COLE'S
## BOOK OF NURSERY RHYMES

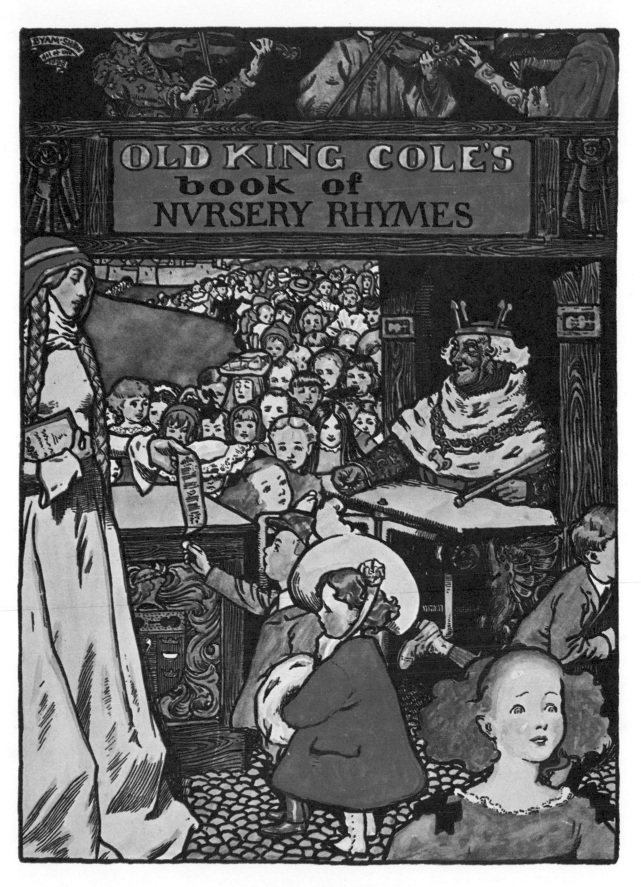

OLD KING COLE'S
book of
NVRSERY RHYMES

Castle Books

Compiled and edited by
FRANK S. OPPEL

Designed by
BARBARA LEVINE

ISBN No. 0-89009-283-4
LIBRARY OF CONGRESS CATALOG No. 79-52642

# TABLE OF CONTENTS

# OLD KING COLE'S
## BOOK OF NURSERY RHYMES

8

# OLD
## KING COLE

OLD King Cole
    Was a merry old soul,
And a merry old soul was he.

HE called for his pipe,
    And he called for his bowl,
    And he called for his fiddlers three.

EVERY fiddler, he had a fiddle,
    And a very fine fiddle had he,

TWEE-TWEEDLE-DEE, tweedle-dee,
    went the fiddlers.
Oh, there's none so rare
    As care compare
With King Cole
    and his fiddlers three.

9

## COME TO BED, SAYS SLEEPY HEAD

COME, let's to bed,
  says Sleepy Head,
Tarry a while, says Slow;
            Put on the pan, says Greedy Nan,
            Let's sup before we go.

## CROSS X PATCH

CROSS X patch,
  Draw the latch,
Sit by the fire and spin:
            Take a cup
            And drink it up,
            Then call the neighbours in.

## PEASE-PUDDING

PEASE-pudding hot,          SOME like it hot,
  Pease-pudding cold,          Some like it cold,
Pease-pudding in the pot    Some like it in the pot,
  Nine days old.              Nine days old.

## THERE WAS AN OLD WOMAN

THERE was an old woman
Lived under a hill;
And if she's not gone,
She lives there still.

11

# OLD MOTHER HUBBARD

OLD Mother Hubbard
    Went to the cupboard
To get her poor Dog a bone;
    But when she came there
The cupboard was bare,
    And so the poor Dog had none.

        SHE went to the baker's
            To buy him some bread,
        But when she came back,
            The poor Dog was dead.

SHE went to the joiner's
    To buy him a coffin,
But when she came back,
    The poor Dog was laughing.

        SHE took a clean dish
            To get him some tripe,
         But when she came back,
            He was smoking a pipe.

SHE went to the ale-house
    To get him some beer,
But when she came back,
    The Dog sat in a chair.

SHE went to the tavern
    For white wine and red,
  But when she came back,
    The Dog stood on his head.

    SHE went to the hatter's,
      To buy him a hat,
      But when she came back,
        He was feeding the cat.

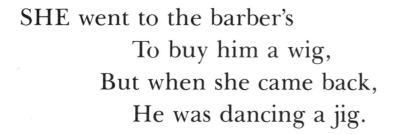

SHE went to the barber's
    To buy him a wig,
  But when she came back,
    He was dancing a jig.

    SHE went to the fruiterer's
      To buy him some fruit,
      But when she came back,
        He was playing the flute.

SHE went to the tailor's
    To buy him a coat,
  But when she came back,
    He was riding a goat.

13

SHE went to the cobbler's
    To buy him some shoes,
    But when she came back,
    He was reading the news.

    SHE went to the sempstress
        To buy him some linen,
        But when she came back,
        The Dog was a-spinning.

SHE went to the hosier's
    To buy him some hose,
    But when she came back,
    He was drest in his clothes.

    THE Dame made a curtsey,
        The Dog made a bow;
        The Dame said, "Your servant,"
        The Dog said, "Bow wow!"

THIS wonderful Dog
    Was Dame Hubbard's delight,
He could sing, he could dance,
    He could read, he could write.
She gave him rich dainties
    Whenever he fed,
And erected a monument
    When he was dead.

## LITTLE FANNY

LITTLE Fanny wears a hat
  Like her ancient Grannie;
Tommy's hoop was
  (think of that!)
Given him by Fanny.

## SEE-SAW-JACK

SEE-SAW-JACK in the hedge,
  Which is the way
to London-bridge?

## RIDE A COCK-HORSE

RIDE a cock-horse
  to Banbury-cross
To see an old lady
  upon a white horse,
Rings on her fingers,
  and bells on her toes,
And so she makes music
  wherever she goes.

# LITTLE
## BO-PEEP

LITTLE Bo-Peep, she lost her sheep,
    And didn't know where to find them;
Let them alone, they'll all come home
    And bring their tails behind them.

    LITTLE Bo-Peep fell fast asleep,
        And dreamt she heard them bleating;
    But when she awoke, she found it a joke,
        For they were still a-fleeting.

THEN up she took her little crook,
    Determined for to find them;
She found them indeed, but it made her heart bleed,
    For they'd left their tails behind them.

    IT happened one day, as Bo-Peep did stray
        Into a meadow hard by,
    There she espied their tails side by side,
        All hung on a tree to dry.

SHE heaved a sigh and wiped her eye,
    Then went o'er hill and dale,
And tried what she could, as a shepherdess should,
    To tack to each sheep its tail.

LITTLE BO-PEEP HAS LOST HER SHEEP

BYAM·SHAW

# HUMPTY-DUMPTY

HUMPTY-DUMPTY sat on a wall,
Humpty-Dumpty had a great fall;
All the king's horses,
and all the king's men
Cannot put Humpty-Dumpty together again.

# LITTLE JACK HORNER

LITTLE Jack Horner
Sat in the corner,
Eating a Christmas pie;

He put in his thumb,
And he took out a plum,
And said,
"What a good boy am I!"

# HICKETY, DICKETY, DOCK

HICKETY, dickety, dock,
The mouse ran up the clock;
The clock struck one,
Down the mouse ran,
Hickety, dickety, dock.

# TO MARKET

TO market, to market,
to buy a fat pig,
Home again, home again,
dancing a jig;
Ride to market to
buy a fat hog,
Home again,
home again, jiggety-jog.

18

## MISTRESS MARY

MISTRESS Mary,
  quite contrary
How does your garden grow?
  With cockle-shells,
and silver bells,
  And pretty maids all in a row.

## BAA, BAA BLACK SHEEP

BAA, baa,
  black sheep,
Have you any wool?
  Yes, marry, have I,
Three bags full;

One for my master,
And one for my dame,
  And one for the little boy
Who lives in the lane.

## THERE WAS AN OLD WOMAN

THERE was an old woman
  who lived in a shoe,
She had so many children
  she didn't know what to do;

She gave them some broth
  with plenty of bread,
She kissed them all fondly
  and sent them to bed.

# GOOSEY, GOOSEY, GANDER

GOOSEY, goosey, gander,
  Where shall I wander?
Up stairs, down stairs,
  And in my lady's chamber;

        There I met an old man
          That would not say his prayers;
        I took him by the left hand,
          And led him down the stairs.

# THERE WERE TWO BLACKBIRDS

THERE were two blackbirds
  Sitting on a hill,
The one named Jack
  The other named Jill;

        FLY away, Jack!
         Fly away, Jill!
        Come again, Jack!
         Come again, Jill!

IF you sneeze on Monday,
  you sneeze for danger;
Sneeze on a Tuesday,
  kiss a stranger;
Sneeze on a Wednesday,
  sneeze for a letter;

Sneeze on a Thursday,
  something better;
Sneeze on a Friday,
  sneeze for sorrow;
Sneeze on a Saturday,
  See your sweetheart to-morrow.

THE man in the moon,
  Came down too soon,
To inquire his way to Norwich.
  He went by the south,
And burnt his mouth
  With eating cold pease porridge.

HARK, hark!
  The dogs do bark,
Beggars are coming to town;
  Some in tags,
Some in rags,
  And some in velvet gowns.

DEEDLE, deedle, dumpling,
  my son John
Went to bed
  with his trousers on

One shoe off,
  the other shoe on,
Deedle, deedle, dumpling,
  my son John.

SNEEZE·ON
MONDAY

SNEEZE
FOR
DANGER

BY·A·M·SHAW
del et inv 1900

23

THERE
WAS·AN
OLD
WOMAN WHO
·RODE·ON·A·BROOM
with a high gee ho
gee humble

·AND·SHE·TOOK·HER·OLD
CAT·BEHIND·FOR·A·GROOM
with a bink lle bumble

24

# THERE WAS AN OLD WOMAN

THERE was an old woman who rode on a broom,
  With a high gee ho, gee humble;

AND she took her old cat behind for a groom,
  With a bimble, bamble, bumble.

BUT the journey so long made them very hungry,
  With a bimble, bamble, bumble.

SAYS Tom, I can find nothing here to eat,
  With a high gee ho, gee humble;

SO let us go back again, I entreat,
  With a bimble, bamble, bumble.

SAYS Tom, I'll go back by myself to our house,
  With a high gee ho, gee humble;

FOR there I can catch a good rat or a mouse,
  With a bimble, bamble, bumble.

BUT, says the old woman, how will you go?
  With a high gee ho, gee humble;

YOU shan't have my nag, I protest and vow,
  With a bimble, bamble, bumble.

NO, no, says Tom, I've a plan of my own;
  With a high gee ho, gee humble;

SO he slid down the rainbow, and left her alone,
  With a bimble, bamble, bumble.

25

PETER PIPER PICKED A PECK OF PICKLED PEPPER

BY A M SHAW

# PETER PIPER

PETER Piper picked
 a peck of pickled pepper;
A peck of pickled pepper
 Peter Piper picked;

    If Peter Piper picked
     a peck of pickled pepper,
     Where's the peck of
      pickled pepper Peter Piper picked?

# WILLY BOY

  WILLY boy, Willy boy,
   where are you going?
  I will go with you,
   if that I may.

            I'm going to the meadow
             to see them a-mowing,
            I'm going to help
             them to make the hay.

# HECTOR PROTECTOR

HECTOR Protector was dressed
 all in green;
Hector Protector was sent
 to the Queen.

            The Queen did not like him,
             nor more did the King;
            So Hector Protector
             was sent back again.

27

# 1, 2,
## BUCKLE MY SHOE

ONE, Two,
　　　Buckle my shoe.

　　　　　　Three, Four,
　　　　　　　　　Open the door.

Five, Six,
　　　Pick up sticks.

　　　　　　Seven, Eight,
　　　　　　　　　Lay them straight.

Nine, Ten,
　　　A good fat hen.

　　　　　　Eleven, Twelve,
　　　　　　　　　Ring the Bell.

Thirteen, Fourteen,
　　　Maids are courting.

　　　Fifteen, Sixteen,
　　　　　　　　　Maids in the Kitchen.

Seventeen, Eighteen,
　　　Maids in waiting.

　　　　　　Nineteen, Twenty,
　　　　　　　　　My plate is empty.

# SING A SONG
## OF SIXPENCE

SING a song of sixpence,
  A pocket full of rye,

  Four and twenty black-birds,
    Baked in a pie

When the pie was open'd
    The birds began to sing

Wasn't that a dainty dish
    To set before the King?

The King was in his counting-house,
    Counting out his money.

 The Queen was in the parlour,
    Eating bread and honey.

The maid was in the garden,
    Hanging out the clothes;

There came a little blackbird,
    And nipp'd off her nose.

29

THIS little pig
went to market;
This little pig
stayed home;
This little pig
ate roast beef;

This little pig
had none;
This little pig
cried, "Wee, wee, wee!
I can't find my way home!"

THE finest,
biggest fish, you see,
Will be the trout
that's caught by me;

But if the monster
will not bite,
Why, then I'll hook
a little mite.

PETER, Peter,
pumpkin-eater,
Had a wife,
and couldn't keep her;

He put her in
a pumpkin-shell,
And there he kept
her very well.

ONCE I saw a little bird,
Come hop, hop, hop;
So I cried, "Little bird,
Will you stop, stop, stop?"

And was going to the window,
To say, "How do you do?"
When he shook his little tail,
And far away he flew.

# LITTLE POLLY FLINDERS

LITTLE Polly Flinders
  Sat among the cinders
Warming her pretty little toes.
            Her mother came and caught her,
            And smacked her little daughter
            For spoiling her nice new clothes.

# POOR ROBIN

THE north wind doth blow,
  And we shall have snow,
And what will poor Robin do then?
  Poor thing!
            He'll sit in a barn,
            And to keep himself warm,
            Will hide his head under his wing,
            Poor thing!

# SHALL I SING?

"SHALL I sing?"
  says the Lark,
"Shall I bloom?"
  says the Flower;
"Shall I come?"
  says the Sun,

"Or shall I?"
  says the shower.
SING your song,
  pretty Bird,
Roses, bloom for an hour;
  Shine on, dearest sun,
  Go away, naughty Shower!

LITTLE POLLY FLINDERS

SAT AMONG THE CINDERS

# A WAS AN ARCHER

A was an Archer, who shot at a frog,
   B was a Butcher, who kept a bull-dog,
C was a Captain, all covered with lace,
   D was a Drummer, who played with much grace.
E was an Esquire, with pride on his brow,
   F was a Farmer, who followed the plough.
G was a Gamester, who had but ill luck,
   H was a Hunter, who hunted a buck.
I was an Italian, who had a white mouse,
   J was a Joiner, who built up a house.
K was a King, so mighty and grand,
   L was a Lady, who had a white hand.
M was a Miser, who hoarded up gold,
   N was a Nobleman, gallant and bold.
O was an Organ boy, who played about town,
   P was a Parson, who wore a black gown.
Q was a Queen, who was fond of her people,
   R was a Robin, who perched on a steeple.
S was a Sailor, who spent all he got,
   T was a Tinker, who mended a pot.
U was an Usher, who loved little boys,
   V was a Veteran, who sold pretty toys.
W was a Watchman, who guarded the door,
   X was expensive, and so became poor.
Y was a Youth, who did not love school,
   Z was a Zany, who looked a great fool.

THREE·WISE MEN OF GOTHAM

36

# THREE WISE MEN
## OF GOTHAM

THREE wise men of Gotham
  Went to sea in a bowl:
If the bowl had been stronger,
  My song had been longer.

# SOLOMON
## GRUNDY

SOLOMON Grundy,
  Born on a Monday,
Christened on Tuesday,
  Married on Wednesday,

Took ill on Thursday,
  Worse on Friday,
Died on Saturday,
  Buried on Sunday;
This is the end
  of Solomon Grundy.

# LITTLE TOMMY
## TITTLEMOUSE

LITTLE Tom Tittlemouse
  lived in a bell-house;
The bell-house broke,
  and Tom Tittlemouse woke.

# ELIZABETH, ELSPETH, BETSY, AND BESS

ELIZABETH, Elspeth, Betsy, and Bess,
They all went together to seek a bird's nest;
They found a bird's nest with five eggs in;
They all took one, and left four in.

# I HAD A LITTLE HOBBY-HORSE

I HAD a
  little hobby-horse,
And it was dapple grey;
  Its head was
made of pea-straw,
  Its tail was made of hay.

I sold it to
  an old woman
For a copper groat,
  And I'll not
sing my song again
  Without a new coat.

# HEY! DIDDLE, DIDDLE

HEY! diddle, diddle,
  The cat and the fiddle,
The cow jumped over the moon;
  The little dog laughed
To see such sport,
  And the dish ran after the spoon.

# POLLY, PUT THE KETTLE ON

POLLY, put the kettle on,
  Polly, put the kettle on,
Polly, put the kettle on,
  And let's drink tea.

Sukey, take it off again,
  Sukey, take it off again,
Sukey, take it off again,
  They've all gone away.

# JACK SPRAT

JACK Sprat would eat no fat,
  His wife would eat no lean;
Was not that a pretty trick
  To make the platter clean?

# WHAT IS TOMMY RUNNING FOR

WHAT is Tommy
  running for,
Running for,
  Running for?
What is Tommy
  running for,
On this fine day?

JIMMY will run
  after Tommy,
After Tommy,
  After Tommy;
That's what Tommy's
  running for,
On this fine day.

# THE LION AND THE UNICORN

THE Lion and the Unicorn,
  Fighting for the Crown;
The Lion beat the Unicorn
  All round the town.

Some gave them white bread,
  Some gave them brown;
Some gave them plum-cake,
  And sent them out of town.

# ROBINSON CRUSOE

POOR old Robinson Crusoe!
  Poor old Robinson Crusoe!
They made him a coat
  Of an old nanny-goat

I wonder how they could do so!
  With a ring-a-ting tang,
  And a ring-a-ting tang,
  Poor old Robinson Crusoe!

# THERE WAS
# AN OLD WOMAN

THERE was an old woman,
  and what do you think?
She lived upon nothing
  but victuals and drink:

Victuals and drink
  were the chief of her diet;
And yet this old woman
  could never be quiet.

THE LION & THE VNICORN FIGHTING FOR THE CROWN

BYAM·SHAW del et inv

ROCK-A-BYE, baby,
on the tree top,
When the wind blows
the cradle will rock,

When the wind lulls,
the cradle will fall,
Down will come baby
and cradle and all.

## VALENTINE

VALENTINE, Oh, Valentine,
Curl your locks as I do mine;
Two before and two behind;
Good-morrow to you, Valentine.

ROCK-A-BYE baby,
Thy cradle is green;
Father's a nobleman,
Mother's a queen,

And Betty's a lady,
And wears a gold ring;
And Johnny's a drummer,
And drums for the King.

I·SAW·THREE SHIPS A-SAILING BY THREE

44

# I SAW THREE SHIPS

I saw three ships come sailing by,
    come sailing by, come sailing by—
I saw three ships come sailing by,
New Year's Day in the morning.

AND what do you think was in them then,
    was in them then, was in them then?
    And what do you think was in them then?
New Year's Day in the morning.

THREE pretty girls were in them then,
    were in them then, were in them then—
    Three pretty girls were in them then,
New Year's Day in the morning.

ONE could whistle and another could sing,
    and the other could play on the violin—
    Such joy was there at my wedding,
New Year's Day in the morning.

## LITTLE MAID

LITTLE maid, little maid,
　Whither goest thou?
Down in the meadow
　To milk my cow.

## DIDDLTY, DUMPTY

DIDDLTY, diddlty, dumpty
　The cat ran up the plum tree;
Give her a plum,
　and down she'll come,
Diddlty, diddlty, dumpty.

## DAFFY-DOWN-DILLY

DAFFY-DOWN-DILLY,
　has come up to town
In a yellow petticoat
　and a green gown.

## LUCY LOCKET

LUCY Locket,
　lost her pocket,
Kitty Fisher found it;
　There was not a penny in it,
But a ribbon round it.

# JOHNNY SHALL HAVE A NEW BONNET

JOHNNY shall
  have a new bonnet,
And Johnny shall
  go to the fair;
And Johnny shall
  have a blue ribbon,
To tie up his
  bonny brown hair.

# JACK BE NIMBLE

JACK be nimble,
  Jack be quick,
And Jack jump over
the candle stick.

# SCHOOL IS OVER

SCHOOL is over,
  Oh, what fun!
Lessons finished,—
  Play begun.
Who'll run fastest,
  You or I?
Who'll laugh loudest?—
  Let us try.

# LITTLE TOM TITTLEMOUSE

LITTLE Tommy Tittlemouse
  Lived in a little house;
He caught fishes,
  In other men's ditches.

THERE was an old woman
  tossed up in a basket
Nineteen times as
  high as the moon;
Where she was going
  I couldn't but ask it,
For in her hand
  she carried a broom.
Old woman, old woman,
  old woman, quoth I,
O whither, O whither
  O whither so high?
To brush the cobwebs
  off the sky!
Shall I go with thee?
  Aye, by-and bye.

## BONNY LASS

BONNY lass, pretty lass,
  Wilt thou be mine?
Thou shall not wash dishes,
  Nor yet serve the swine;
Thou shalt sit on a cushion,
  and sew a fine seam,
And thou shalt eat strawberries,
  sugar and cream!

## GIRLS AND BOYS COME OUT TO PLAY

GIRLS and boys
  come out to play,
The moon it shines
  as bright as day;
Leave your supper,
  and leave your sleep,
And come to your
  playmates in the street;

Come with a whoop,
  Come with a call,
Come with a good will,
  Or come not at all;
Up the ladder
  and down the wall,
A halfpenny loaf
  will serve us all.

## I SAW A SHIP

I SAW a ship
  that sailed the sea,
It left me as the
  sun went down;
The white birds flew,
  and followed it
To town,—to London town.

RIGHT sad were
  we to stand alone,
And see it pass
  so far away;
And yet we knew
  some ship would come—
Some other ship—
  some other day.

49

# THREE BLIND MICE

THREE blind mice,
See how they run!
They all ran after
the farmer's wife,
Who cut off their tails
with a carving knife.
Did you ever see
such a thing in your life
As three blind mice?

# THREE LITTLE KITTENS

THREE little kittens
they lost their mittens,
And they began to cry,
"Oh! mammy dear,
We sadly fear,
Our mittens we have lost!"
"What! lost your mittens,
You naughty kittens,
Then you shall have no pie."
Miew, miew, miew, miew,
Miew, miew, miew, miew.

THE three little kittens
they found their mittens,
And they began to cry,
"Oh! mammy dear,
See here, see here,
Our mittens we have found."
"What! found your mittens,
You little kittens,
Then you shall have some pie."
Purr, purr, purr, purr,
Purr, purr, purr, purr.

THREE
BLIND
MICE

BYAM·SHAW
1901

51

SIMPLE SIMON MET A PIE-MAN

GOING·TO·THE·FAIR

BYAM SHAW 1901

SIMPLE Simon met a pieman,
    Going to the fair:
    Says Simple Simon to the pieman,
"Let me taste your ware."

    SAYS the pieman to Simple Simon,
        "Show me first your penny."
    Says Simple Simon to the pieman,
"Indeed I have not any."

SIMPLE Simon went a-fishing
    For to catch a whale;
    All the water he had got
Was in his mother's pail.

    SIMPLE Simon went to look
        If plums grew on a thistle;
    He pricked his fingers very much,
Which made poor Simon whistle.

## LADY QUEEN ANNE

QUEEN Anne, Queen Anne,
  she sits in the sun,
As fair as the lily,
  as white as the swan:
I send you three letters,
  so pray you read one.
I cannot read one
  unless I read all;
So pray, Master Teddy,
  deliver the ball.

## LITTLE WIND

LITTLE wind,
  blow on the hill-top,
Little wind,
  blow down the plain;
Little wind,
  blow up the sunshine,
Little wind,
  blow off the rain.

## ELSIE MARLEY

ELSIE MARLEY has grown so fine,
  She won't get up to serve the swine;
But lies in bed till eight or nine,
  And surely she does take her time.

## HERE AM I

HERE am I, little jumping Joan,
  When nobody's with me,
I'm always alone.

LADY DD QVEEN ANNE

SHE·SITS
IN·THE
SVN

BYAM·SHAW
1901

55

## RAIN, RAIN, GO AWAY

RAIN, rain, go away,
Come again another day;
Little Arthur wants to play.

## PIPPIN HILL

AS I was going
up Pippin Hill,
Pippin Hill was dirty;
There I met a sweet pretty
And she dropped me a curtsey.

## ONE FOOT UP

ONE foot up,
the other foot down,
That's the way
to London-town.

## TOMMY SNOOKS

AS Tommy Snooks
and Bessie Brooks
Were walking out one Sunday;
Says Tommy Snooks
to Bessie Brooks,
"To-morrow will be Monday."

# RIDE, BABY, RIDE

RIDE, baby, ride,
  Pretty baby shall ride,
And have a little puppy-dog
  tied to her side,
And little pussy-cat
  tied to the other,

And away she shall ride
  to see her grandmother,
To see her grandmother,
  To see her grandmother.

# RING-A-RING-A-ROSIES

RING-a-ring-a-roses,
  A pocket full of posies;
Hush! hush! hush! hush!
  We're all tumbled down.

# THREE TABBIES

THREE tabbies took
  out their cats to tea,
As well-behaved tabbies
  as well could be;
Each sat in the chair
  that each preferred,

    They mewed for their milk,
      and they sipped and purred.
    Now tell me this
      (as these cats you've seen them)—
    How many lives
      had these cats between them?

# LITTLE MISS MUFFET

LITTLE Miss Muffet,
  She sat on a tuffet,
Eating of curds and whey;
  There came a great spider,
Who sat down beside her,
  And frightened Miss Muffet away.

# LITTLE BOY BLUE

LITTLE Boy Blue,
  come blow up your horn,
The sheep's in the meadow,
  the cow's in the corn.

# JACK AND JILL

JACK and Jill
  went up the hill,
To fetch a pail of water;
  Jack fell down,
And broke his crown,
  and Jill came tumbling after.

LITTLE MISS
MVFFET

BYAM·SHAW
1901

59

## BARBER, BARBER, SHAVE A PIG

BARBER, barber, shave a pig,
  How many hairs will make a wig?
"Four-and-twenty, that's enough."
  Give the barber a pinch of snuff.

## PUSSY-CAT, PUSSY-CAT

PUSSY-CAT, pussy-cat,
  where have you been?
I've been to London
  to look at the Queen.

Pussy-cat, pussy-cat,
  what did you there?
I frightened a little mouse
  under the chair.

## COCK A DOODLE DOO

COCK a doodle doo!
  My dame has lost her shoe;
My master's lost
  his fiddling-stick,
And don't know what to do.

## I LIKE LITTLE PUSSY

I LIKE little pussy,
  her coat is so warm,
And if I don't hurt her
  she'll do me no harm;

So I'll not pull her tail,
  nor drive her away,
But pussy and I
  very gently will play.

# PAT-A-CAKE

PAT-A-CAKE, pat-a-cake,
  baker's man!
So I will, master,
  as fast as I can:
Pat it, and prick it,
  and mark it with T,
Put in the oven for Tommy and me.

# GREAT A

GREAT A, little a,
  Bouncing B!
The cat's in the cup-board,
  And she can't see.

# 1, 2, 3, 4, 5

1, 2, 3, 4, 5!
  I caught a hare alive;
6, 7, 8, 9, 10!
  I let her go again.

# A. B. C.

A. B. C. tumble down D,
  The cat's in the cupboard
and can't see me.

63

# I HAD A LITTLE HUSBAND

I had a
  little husband,
no bigger than my thumb;
  I put him in a pint pot,
and there I bid him drum.
  I bought a little horse,
that galloped up and down;
            I bridled him, and saddled him,
      and sent him out of town.
      I gave him some garters,
  to garter up his hose;
      And a little handkerchief,
  to wipe his pretty nose.

# I MET
# A LASS

AS I stepped out          She'd shoes with strings,
  to hear the news,          and a friend had tied them,
I met a lass              She'd a nice little pair
  in socks and shoes;      of feet inside them!

# THERE WAS A CROOKED MAN

THERE was a crooked man,
  and he went a crooked mile,
He found a crooked sixpence
  against a crooked stile;
            He bought a crooked cat,
              which caught a crooked mouse,
            And they all lived together
              in a little crooked house.

# MARY HAD
## A LITTLE LAMB

MARY had a little lamb,
Its fleece was white as snow;

And everywhere that Mary went,
The lamb was sure to go.

He followed her to school one day;
That was against the rule;

It made the children laugh and play
To see a lamb at school.

And so the teacher turned him out,
But still he lingered near,

And waited patiently about,
Till Mary did appear.

"What makes the lamb love Mary so?"
The eager children cry.

 "Oh, Mary loves the lamb, you know,"
The teacher did reply.

# THE QUEEN OF HEARTS

THE Queen of Hearts,
  she made some tarts,
All on a summer's day;
  The Knave of Hearts,
He stole the tarts,
  and took them clean away.

The King of Hearts
  called for the tarts,
And beat the Knave full sore;
  The Knave of Hearts
Brought back the tarts,
  and vowed he'd steal no more.

# LITTLE TOM TUCKER

LITTLE Tom Tucker
  Sings for his supper,
What shall he eat?
  White bread and butter.

# A DILLER, A DOLLAR

A DILLER, a dollar,
  A ten o'clock scholar,
What makes you come so soon?
  You used to come at ten o'clock,
But now you come at noon.

# THE ROSE IS RED

THE rose is red,
  The violet's blue,
Sugar is sweet,
  And so are you.

## HERE GOES MY LORD

HERE goes my lord
  A trot, a trot, a trot, a trot;
Here goes my lady
  A canter, a canter, a canter, a canter!
Here goes my young master
  Jockey-hitch, Jockey-hitch,
Jockey-hitch, Jockey-hitch;
  Here goes my young miss,
An amble, an amble, an amble, an amble!

## SHOE THE HORSE

SHOE the horse
  and shoe the mare;
But let the little
  colt go bare.

## IF WISHES WERE HORSES

IF wishes were horses,
  Beggars would ride;
If turnips were watches,
  I would wear one by my side.

## DOCTOR FOSTER

DOCTOR Foster went to Glo'ster
  In a shower of rain;
He stepped in a puddle,
  up to the middle,
And never went there again.

HERE · GOES ·
MY · LORD
A · TROT · A · TROT
A · TROT · A · TROT

BYAM · SHAW
1901

69

## THE MULBERRY BUSH

HERE we go round
  the mulberry-bush,
The mulberry-bush,
  the mulberry-bush;
Here we go round
  the mulberry-bush
On a sunshiny morning.

THIS is the way
  we wash our clothes,
Wash our clothes,
  wash our clothes;
This is the way
  we wash our clothes
On a cold frosty morning!

## HOT-CROSS BUNS

HOT-cross Buns!
  Hot-cross Buns!
One a penny, two a penny.
  Hot-cross Buns!

HOT-cross Buns!
  Hot-cross Buns!
If ye have no daughters
  Give them to your sons.

## THIRTY DAYS HATH SEPTEMBER

THIRTY days hath September,
  April, June, and November;
February has twenty-eight alone,
  All the rest have thirty-one,

Excepting Leap year,
  that's the time
When February's days
  are twenty-nine.

## RIDE A COCK-HORSE

RIDE a cock-horse
  to Banbury Cross,
To buy little Johnny
  a galloping horse;

It trots behind,
  and it ambles before,
And Johnny shall ride
  till he can ride no more.

## TOM, TOM, THE PIPER'S SON

TOM, Tom, the piper's son,
  Stole a pig, and away he run;
The pig was eat, and Tom was beat,
  And Tom ran roaring
down the street.

## LITTLE FRED

WHEN little Fred went to bed
  He always said his prayers.
He kissed mamma and then papa,
  And straight-way went upstairs.

## LITTLE WILLIE WINKLE

LITTLE Willie Winkle
  runs through the town,
Upstairs and downstairs,
  in his nightgown,

Rapping at the window,
  crying through the lock,
"Are the children in their beds?
  for now it's eight o'clock."

# FOUR-AND-TWENTY TAILORS

FOUR-and-twenty tailors
  went to catch a snail,
The best man amongst them
  durst not touch her tail;
She put out her horns,
  like a little Kyloe cow,
Run, tailors, run,
  or she'll kill you all just now.

# AS I WENT TO BONNER

AS I went to Bonner,
  I met a pig without a wig,
Upon my word and honor.

# IF I'D AS MUCH MONEY

IF I'd as much money
  as I could spend,
I never would cry
  old chairs to mend;

Old chairs to mend,
  old chairs to mend,
I never would cry
  old chairs to mend.

FOUR AND TWENTY TAILORS WENT·TO CATCH·A SNAIL

BYAM·SHAW

# IF ALL THE WORLD WERE WATER

IF all the world were water,
  And all the water were ink,
What should we do
  for bread and cheese?
What should we do for drink?

# THE WIND

WHEN the wind
  is in the east,
'Tis neither good
  for man nor beast;
When the wind
  is in the north,
The skilful fisher
  goes not forth;

When the wind is
  in the south,
It blows the bait
  in the fishes' mouth;
When the wind is
  in the west,
Then 'tis at
  the very best.

# HUB A DUB DUB

HUB a dub dub,
  Three men in a tub;
And who do you think they be?
  The butcher, the baker,
The candlestick maker;
  Turn 'em out knaves all three!

# WHEN I WAS
## A LITTLE BOY

WHEN I was a little boy
  I lived by myself;
And all the bread
  and cheese I got
I put upon the shelf.

THE rats and the mice
  They made such a strife,
I was forced
  to go to London town
To buy me a wife.

THE streets were so broad,
  And the lanes were so narrow,
I was forced to bring my wife home
  In a wheelbarrow.

THE wheelbarrow broke,
  And my wife had a fall,
Down came wheelbarrow,
  Wife and all.

# A HAPPY CHILD AM I

MY house is red—
  a little house,
A happy child am I,
  I laugh and play
the livelong day
  I hardly ever cry.

I HAVE a tree,
  a green, green tree,
To shade me from the sun;
  And under it I often sit,
When all my work is done.

MY little basket
  I will take,
And trip into the town;
  When next I'm there
I'll buy some cake,
  And spend my
bright half-crown.

# THE MAN IN THE WILDERNESS

THE man in the
  wilderness asked me,
How many strawberries
  grew in the sea?

I answered him
  as I thought good,
As many as red herrings
  grew in the wood.

# A CARRION CROW
## SAT ON AN OAK

Carrion Crow sat on an oak,
        Derry, derry, derry, decco;
A carrion crow sat on an oak,
Watching a tailor shape a coat.
        Heigh-ho! the carrion crow,
Derry, derry, derry, decco.
        "O wife, bring me my old bent bow,"
                Derry, derry, derry, decco;
        "O wife, bring me my old bent bow,
"That I may shoot yon carrion crow."
        Heigh-ho! the carrion crow,
        Derry, derry, derry, decco.
THE tailor shot, and he missed his mark,
        Derry, derry, derry, decco;
        The tailor shot, and he missed his mark,
And shot his old sow right through the heart.
        Heigh-ho! the carrion crow,
Derry, derry, derry, decco.
        "O wife, bring brandy in a spoon,"
                Derry, derry, derry, decco;
        "O wife, bring brandy in a spoon,
"For our old sow is in a swoon."
                Heigh-ho! the carrion crow,
        Derry, derry, derry, decco.

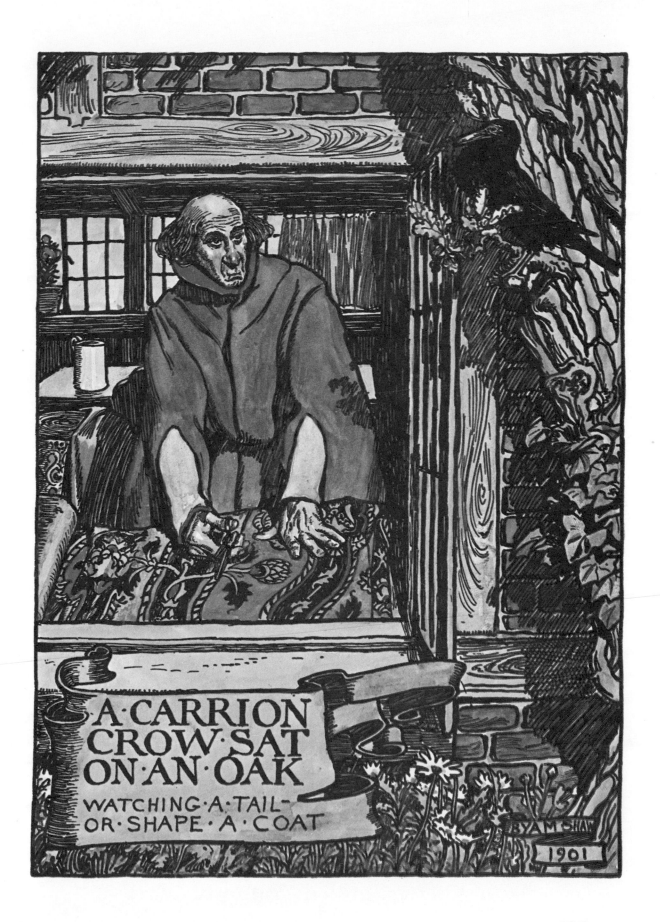

A·CARRION
CROW·SAT
ON·AN·OAK
WATCHING·A·TAIL-
OR·SHAPE·A·COAT

BYAM·SHAW
1901

79

## TO MARKET

TO market, to market,
  To buy a plum bun;
Home again, come again,
  Market is done.

## DING, DONG BELL

DING, dong bell,
  Pussy's in the well!
Who put her in?
  Little Tommy Lin.
Who pulled her out?—
  Dog with long snout.

## DIDDLTY, DUMPTY

DIDDLEDY, diddledy, dumpty:
  The cat ran up the plum-tree.
I'll lay you a crown
  I'll fetch you down;
So diddledy, diddledy, dumpty.